THE MORE THAN 52 CHURCHES WORKBOOK

PURSUE CHRISTIAN COMMUNITY AND GROW
IN OUR FAITH

VISITING CHURCHES SERIES

PETER DEHAAN

The More Than 52 Churches Workbook: Pursue Christian Community and Grow in Our Faith © 2020 by Peter DeHaan.

Visiting Churches Series

All rights reserved: No part of this book may be reproduced, disseminated, or transmitted in any form, by any means, or for any purpose without the express written consent of the author or his legal representatives. The only exception is the cover image and short excerpts for reviews or academic research. For permissions: PeterDeHaan.com/contact.

Scriptures taken from the Holy Bible, New International Version®, NIV®. Copyright © 1973, 1978, 1984, 2011 by Biblica, Inc.™ Used by permission of Zondervan. All rights reserved worldwide. www.zondervan.com The "NIV" and "New International Version" are trademarks registered in the United States Patent and Trademark Office by Biblica, Inc.™

Published by Rock Rooster Books, Grand Rapids, Michigan

ISBNs:

- 978-1-948082-41-9 (e-book)
- 978-1-948082-42-6 (paperback)
- 978-1-948082-43-3 (hardcover)

Credits:

- Developmental editor: Cathy Rueter
- Copy editor: Robyn Mulder
- Cover design: Taryn Nergaard
- Author photo: Chelsie Jensen Photography

To all who seek spiritual community and want to grow in their faith.

Books in the Visiting Churches Series:

52 Churches

More Than 52 Churches

Visiting Online Church

Shopping for Church

The 52 Churches Workbook

The More Than 52 Churches Workbook

For a list of all Peter's books, go to

PeterDeHaan.com/books

CONTENTS

Wasn't 52 Churches Enough?   1
Church #53: Home for Easter Sunday   4

PART 1
More Opportunities

Church #54: Emergent Maybe   13
Church #55: New and Small   18
Church #56: The Reboot   23
Church #57: Another New Church   28
Church #58: Not So Friendly   33
Church #59: Big, Yet Compelling   38
Church #60: A Missed Opportunity   43
Church #61: The Wrong Time to Visit   46
Church #62: Off to a Great Start   51
Church #63: We Don't Need No Sermon   56
Church #64: Is Bigger Always Better?   61
Church #65: Short of Meeting Expectations   66
Church #66, Part 1: Gifts of the Spirit   71
Church #66, Part 2: A Normal Service   76
Church #67: Satellite Church   81
Church #68: Urban on a Mission   88

PART 2
Other Considerations

Church #69: Suffering from a Bad Rap   97
Church #70: Unplanned and Spontaneous   100
Church #71: A Messianic Jewish Congregation   103
Church #72: Respected and Esteemed   106
Church #73: A Debatable Destination   109

Church #74: An Intriguing Mystery	112
Church #75: Fatigue and Fear Set In	115
Our Home Church	118
Bonus Content: How to Be an Engaging Church	122
Bonus Content: How to Go to Church	133
The Next Steps	139
Which Book Do You Want to Read Next?	142
About Peter DeHaan	143
Books by Peter DeHaan	145

WASN'T 52 CHURCHES ENOUGH?

For *52 Churches*, my wife and I spent one year visiting a different Christian church every week. What we learned was amazing. Still, I knew the journey wasn't over. We had more to do and visited more churches. I shared these new experiences in *More Than 52 Churches*.

Now let's dig deeper with this workbook.

Visiting churches wore us down. Visitors to our churches may share a similar perspective. *What can we do to help weary visitors experience God and enjoy community?*

_____

_____

_____

_____

_____

_____

Each church's worship practices varied, and their theology diverged, but the God behind them stands constant. *How can we keep our focus on God and not on our church service and theology?*

_____

_____

_____

_____

_____

_____

A slight majority of the population are introverts who may struggle more in visiting churches. *Regardless of where we are on the introvert-extrovert scale, what can we do to personally embrace church visitors?*

_____

_____

_____

_____

_____

_____

_____

CHURCH #53: HOME FOR EASTER SUNDAY

As a reference, I share attending our home church on Easter Sunday. This marks the end of *52 Churches* and the start of *More Than 52 Churches*. Though I strive to remain objective in visiting churches, our home church forms the lens I look through.

I see value in worshiping God with family, and for Easter we go with our children and their spouses. *What can we do to attend church and celebrate Jesus with our family?*

_____

_____

_____

_____

_____

_____

The 150-year-old building, even with many improvements, still feels dated. *What can we do to make our church facility as conducive to worship and community as possible?*

_____

_____

_____

_____

_____

_____

Though the shortcomings of a worship space shouldn't block us from God, they can. *How can we minimize the cumbersome facility elements we can't change so they don't get in the way of us encountering God?*

_____

_____

_____

_____

_____

_____

There's no plan for the service, only a general intent. The Holy Spirit will guide the leaders in what to do and for how long. *How much of a role do we let the Holy Spirit play in our church services?*

_____

_____

_____

_____

_____

_____

Though we were gone for a year, I listened to the messages online. *In what ways can we extend the church worship experience and teaching to those who can't attend in person?*

_____

_____

_____

_____

_____

_____

Baptism at churches varies from a reserved rite, to a public declaration of faith, to an enthusiastic celebration. *What can we do to better embrace baptism as the early church did in the Bible?*

_____

_____

_____

_____

_____

_____

As we leave the building ninety minutes later, some are already arriving for the second service. *Not looking at efficiency, but focusing on the human aspect, how can we foster a better transition between services?*

_____

_____

_____

_____

_____

_____

PART 1

MORE OPPORTUNITIES

We list churches we wanted to visit for *52 Churches* but couldn't. We also look for churches that will give us greater variety in terms of size and service style. We can pick from hundreds of options. With numerous possibilities to consider we must choose carefully.

We're willing to drive farther to explore greater variations in Jesus's church because that is our goal. *How far are we comfortable traveling to visit a church?*

_____

_____

_____

_____

_____

_____

Though we are willing to intentionally drive quite a distance to visit a church once, we don't want to do so every week. *How far should we be willing to travel every week to go to church?*

_____

_____

_____

_____

_____

_____

Attending a nearby church increases the potential of worshiping with neighbors. *How can we balance going to the church of our preference with attending a church in our community with neighbors?*

_____

_____

_____

_____

_____

_____

_____

CHURCH #54: EMERGENT MAYBE

I've read books about emergent churches, but I've never been to one. At this church, the church leaders want to serve this underserved neighborhood: the poorest and least safe, crime-laden and hopeless.

They meet at 5:30 p.m. The plan is to share a meal, offer a brief teaching, and go for a prayer walk in the neighborhood. *How open are we to go to church Sunday evening instead of Sunday morning?*

_____

_____

_____

_____

_____

_____

My wife, Candy, asks what food to bring. As visitors, they'd forgive us if we showed up empty-handed, but during *52 Churches* we did our share of mooching. *How open are we to include people in our potluck who have nothing to contribute?*

_____

_____

_____

_____

_____

_____

Our leader says that sharing a meal is Communion. As we eat and drink together, we do so to remember Jesus. *How open are we to embrace Communion as a meal and a meal as Communion?*

_____

_____

_____

_____

_____

_____

The sanctuary lights remain off, with mood lighting taking their place. It provides a peaceful, subdued setting. Some women dance in the back with graceful movement. *What role can we let dance play in our worship experience?*

_____

_____

_____

_____

_____

Some children wave worship flags, praising God through solemn movement. Other kids play quiet games, build with foam blocks, or create art on a wall-sized chalkboard. *How can we include our children in worship? What if their worship differs from ours?*

_____

_____

_____

_____

_____

The service ends, but no one leaves. We chat with several people, offering prayers and blessings as needed. *After the service officially ends, how can we embrace community and minister to others?*

_____

_____

_____

_____

_____

I think we just had our first emergent church experience. *Does our church do things differently to better meet the needs of the people we want to reach? If not, what must change?*

CHURCH #55: NEW AND SMALL

After *52 Churches* ended, a new church launched in our area. Their primary marketing was yard signs, which promoted a fresh approach to church. With a last-minute opening in our schedule, we have an opportunity to visit.

Their Facebook page contains recent updates, but they don't mention service times or a schedule beyond their first two meetings several months ago. *What can we do to make sure we provide potential visitors with up-to-date information?*

_____

_____

_____

_____

_____

_____

They call themselves nondenominational, but their website —which Candy eventually finds—describes a church that sounds most evangelical. Why not just say they're evangelical? *Do the labels we use for our church accurately reflect who we are?*

_____

_____

_____

_____

_____

We're the oldest people present, with kids, teens, and younger adults all represented. After visiting many churches with older congregations, this is a pleasant change. *What age groups does our church cater to? What does this say about our focus and future?*

_____

_____

_____

_____

_____

They start fifteen minutes late. I'm not sure if this is their norm or because of harsh weather. *When does our church service actually begin? What does this communicate to visitors?*

_____

_____

_____

_____

_____

At many churches a time of sharing approaches gossip or bragging. Not so here. The pain they share is not just a lament but also a testimony, teaching and encouraging others. *How can we publicly share our needs and still edify the church?*

_____

_____

_____

_____

_____

They tell us many members have a charismatic background, but they're careful to avoid excess, following Paul's teaching (1 Corinthians 14:27–28). *How can we better ground our church in what the Bible teaches?*

_____

_____

_____

_____

_____

Their leader follows Paul's example of working his trade to provide for ministry (Acts 18:2–3). I like not expecting paid clergy to serve members but for members to minister to each other. *How well do we do at ministering to one another?*

CHURCH #56: THE REBOOT

During *52 Churches*, two churches planned to simultaneously shut down for a few months and then reopen as a new, merged entity. But it took much longer. At last we can visit. I call this process a reboot.

The large parking lot has ample room. People mill about outside, including two greeters, bantering with all who pass. One opens the door for us. *What initial impression does our church make when people arrive?*

_____

_____

_____

_____

I've been in this building before. Gone are the pews, organ, and formal elements. In their place are padded chairs and a contemporary altar. What once approached stodgy is now chic. Subdued lighting adds to the allure. *What is our sanctuary's ambience? What should change?*

_____

_____

_____

_____

_____

Communion is open to "anyone who acknowledges Jesus Christ as the risen Savior." Children are welcome to take part, too, as determined by their parents or caregivers. *How well does our church convey Communion expectations?*

_____

_____

_____

_____

_____

It's Mother's Day, and they distribute carnations to every female, "honoring all women." This nicely avoids the risk of inadvertently disregarding those who desperately long to be moms but aren't, can't, or once were. *What changes should our churches make to be more inclusive?*

_____

_____

_____

_____

_____

The children come forward for a blessing. The pastor says, "Let's talk to Jesus." I appreciate his simple, kid-appropriate reminder of what prayer is. *What can we do to keep our faith practices fresh?*

_____

_____

_____

_____

_____

_____

The minister says, "Giving is an act of worship." As a teen I assumed this was a euphemism for "give us your money." Now it clicks with me. *How can we better connect our giving with our worship?*

_____

_____

_____

_____

_____

_____

Despite updates to the sanctuary, the service unfolds like most others. They merely house typical expectations in a new package. *Are our church's attempts to be relevant mere show or significant?*

_____

_____

_____

_____

_____

_____

_____

CHURCH #57: ANOTHER NEW CHURCH

During our *52 Churches* journey, many people suggested we visit today's destination, but it was too far away. When the building's former occupants became too few to carry on, another church took over the building and launched a new gathering.

A sign in the drive, too small to easily read, directs traffic in two directions. Unable to read it without stopping, I guess. *Do we need to rework our church signs so that they actually help?*

_____

_____

_____

_____

_____

_____

After we enter, the worship team begins playing to start the service. This church has a reputation for its many talented musicians, and we're seeing the results. *What is our church's reputation? What do we need to improve?*

_____

_____

_____

_____

_____

_____

A leader asks us to break into groups and discuss the purpose of church. We're nicely started when she tells everyone to wrap things up. *What is the purpose of church? How should it function to meet this intent?*

_____

_____

_____

_____

_____

_____

With their minister gone, the intern fills in. He shares a string of Bible verses and intriguing soundbites, but I fail to grasp their connection with the purpose of church. *What should we do when the message falls short?*

_____

_____

_____

_____

_____

_____

The worship team plays softly to end the service, while the prayer team comes forward to pray for those who seek prayer. *How open are we to pray for others at church? And away from church?*

_____

_____

_____

_____

_____

_____

When the music starts for the second service, we hustle out of the sanctuary and leave. *How can we allow more time for people to experience community after the service and not shoo them away?*

_____

_____

_____

_____

_____

_____

Both before and after the service we had rich interaction with people we knew. But I wonder about our reception had no one known us. *How can we make our pre-church and post-church interaction more inclusive of people we don't know?*

CHURCH #58: NOT SO FRIENDLY

The website of this large church boasts that we'll find "a warm and friendly group of people." If you must claim you're friendly, you might not be. Experience tells me they'll try but will fall short.

Always anxious before visiting a church, my gut churns even more. A sharp pain jolts me. My heart thumps. I later learn I had an anxiety attack. *How can we best help people who struggle to enter a church building?*

_____

_____

_____

_____

_____

_____

Inside, preoccupied people mill about. We walk slowly, giving someone time to approach us. No one does. And we see no one for us to approach. *How can we be more aware of people longing for interaction?*

_____

_____

_____

_____

_____

_____

When the countdown timer reaches zero the worship team begins to lead us in song. Most of the people, however, aren't ready to worship. They aren't even sitting down. *How can we better prepare ourselves to worship God?*

_____

_____

_____

_____

_____

As I settle into the chorus of an unfamiliar tune, a reunion between two people hijacks my focus. Their loud conversation distracts me well into the third song. *How can we balance a desire for community with the goal of worship?*

_____

_____

_____

_____

_____

We end up with about three hundred people, half of whom wander in several minutes after the service starts. *How can we make sure we arrive on time and not distract others from experiencing God?*

_____

_____

_____

_____

_____

The minister leads us in Communion. "Everyone is invited to the table to encounter Jesus in their own way." This is most inclusive. *How can we better include people and help them encounter Jesus?*

_____

_____

_____

_____

_____

The insightful message was worth the hour-and-forty-five-minute service, but the rest disappointed me. I didn't worship God today or experience community. I walk out feeling lonely. *What can we do to make sure people don't leave church disappointed or ignored?*

_____

_____

_____

_____

_____

_____

_____

CHURCH #59: BIG, YET COMPELLING

One of the area's megachurches has intrigued me for years. I once wanted to be part of it. Now I'm not sure. Our first visit came several years ago, long before the original *52 Churches* project. Now we return for a fresh look.

As we drive to their facility, I pray for our time there, what we will learn, and what God wants to teach us. *Do we remember to pray before church? What is the focus of our prayers?*

_____

_____

_____

_____

_____

_____

An usher hands me a bulletin. This isn't an usher-and-bulletin church. The paper states "Advent Liturgy." This certainly isn't a liturgical congregation. *How can we engage in a service if it's different than what we expect?*

_____

_____

_____

_____

_____

The subdued playing lacks the excitement I anticipated. They teach us a song in Latin. The timing befuddles me. The words perplex me. *When the music doesn't click, how can we push through and worship God anyway?*

I assume the liturgy, restrained playing, and song are something different they're doing for Advent: changing the familiar into something with a mystical aura. *What can we do to breathe freshness into our adoration of Jesus?*

During the greeting time we have brief interactions with those sitting around us. But, unable to move, we then stand writhing in awkward isolation while conversations abound around us. *How can we best greet those who need it most?*

_____

_____

_____

_____

_____

I suspect this Sunday's teaching is typical and the rest of the service is not. Somber music pulls me down, while liturgy pushes me away. I must work to embrace all forms of worship. *How can we help people overcome barriers to encountering God?*

_____

_____

_____

_____

_____

"I loved the teaching," I tell Candy, "but I don't have the energy to try to plug into a large church." *How can we help people plug into our church without making them work too hard?*

_____

_____

_____

_____

_____

_____

CHURCH #60: A MISSED OPPORTUNITY

I meet a pastor launching a church in an underserved urban area. Her dream is a church for people of all ages, races, and backgrounds—a colorful mosaic of folks seeking to grow together in Jesus under Holy Spirit power.

Her vision draws me in. Being part of this church is not inconceivable, even though it's thirty minutes away. *How open are we to be part of God's great adventure when it's not convenient?*

Months later their website still casts a vision for a downtown church, but details appear for a suburban service, without mentioning one downtown. Did their vision change? *How can we keep our plans and vision aligned with God's leading?*

I assume they've given up on reaching the downtown urban area. Just like many other well-intentioned folks, they seem content in the suburbs. Most people are. *Are we content to remain where we're comfortable and with those we know?*

_____

_____

_____

_____

_____

_____

_____

CHURCH #61: THE WRONG TIME TO VISIT

Many Sundays we've driven by this church, noting a three-quarters-full lot for their first service and a packed one for their second. While church size doesn't impress me and growth may be misleading, both *can* signal spiritual vitality. I'm intrigued.

Candy is gone, so I'm on my own. I'm okay visiting a church by myself, but staying home is so tempting. *How can we form a habit of regular church attendance? How can we stick with it?*

_____

_____

_____

_____

_____

_____

The parking lot has plenty of space. I'm underwhelmed. *What message does our parking lot send? How can we make parking be a positive and inviting introduction to our facility?*

_____

_____

_____

_____

_____

_____

Being alone, I feel more exposed than usual. I pause, hoping someone will greet me. No one does. And no one's available for me to approach. Visiting a church solo takes extra courage. *How can we welcome a person squirming in silence?*

_____

_____

_____

_____

_____

_____

Several minutes after it's time to start, the worship team begins playing. Their opening strains call people into the sanctuary. These late arrivals distract me from worship. *How can we make sure we don't impede others from experiencing God?*

_____

_____

_____

_____

_____

_____

Next is the greeting. Epic fail. I'm weary of these trivial attempts at connection: people faking friendly when ordered and then withdrawing. *How can we be open and friendly all the time and not just when instructed?*

_____

_____

_____

_____

_____

_____

The senior pastor is gone, with a second-year seminarian filling in. The guy is green. He should practice in seminary, not on a congregation. *When a message falls short—which will inevitably happen—how should we respond?*

_____

_____

_____

_____

_____

I leave frustrated. I enjoyed the music, but the message caused consternation, and the lack of connection left me empty. Was it my fault or theirs? *How can we help others leave church feeling better than when they arrived?*

CHURCH #62: OFF TO A GREAT START

It's a nondenominational church plant, with the sending congregation residing several states away. It's curious that an out-of-state church would launch a ministry in an area noted for its religious reputation, with "a church on every corner."

They meet in a school building, providing a more approachable, less intimidating environment for unchurched people. *What is our perspective for having church in a traditional space? How open are we for a more visitor-friendly alternative?*

_____

_____

_____

_____

_____

_____

When we arrive, a man standing at the parking lot's edge greets us with enthusiasm. What a wonderful welcome. *How aware are we that creating a good first impression occurs before people walk inside?*

_____

_____

_____

_____

_____

_____

Another man greets us, opening the door with a gracious flourish. The friendly reception of these two men is infectious. I can't wait to experience church here. *What can we do to build anticipation for our church services?*

_____

_____

_____

_____

_____

_____

To start the service they welcome everyone, asking first-time visitors to raise their hands. Many do. Normally I hate this practice, but with many visitors, I don't feel singled out. *How can we celebrate visitors without making them squirm?*

_____

_____

_____

_____

_____

_____

When the associate pastor announces the offering, he stresses it's only for regulars, not visitors. This helps counter the common criticism that churches only want our money. *Which example does our church follow?*

_____

_____

_____

_____

_____

"We need to attack the lie that you can have it all," the teaching pastor says. "It's not possible. Something needs to give." *How can we find God-honoring contentment? How can we encourage others to do the same?*

_____

_____

_____

_____

_____

The More Than 52 Churches Workbook

Despite the many churches in the area, the evident excitement and impressive attendance at this church suggests there's room for one more. *Should we associate church attendance and growth rates with God's approval? Or might size be our perspective?*

_____

_____

_____

_____

_____

_____

_____

CHURCH #63: WE DON'T NEED NO SERMON

When Candy started a new job, she learned one of her coworkers goes to a church near the one we normally attend. With a non-church sounding name, I'm intrigued. We decide to visit.

As we drive to this church, I'm so glad for a reprieve from ours and the pointless lectures I endure for the sake of community. Even so, I'll miss seeing the people there. *Should the focus of church be on the message or on community?*

_____

_____

_____

_____

_____

_____

Once inside the building we weave our way through people, all engaged in conversation with friends—and too busy to notice us. *How do we respond when we see someone we don't know? How should we react?*

_____

_____

_____

_____

_____

_____

In the sanctuary, Candy spots her coworker and waves. His face beams. He beckons us. "I'm so glad you're here." He is truly overjoyed to see us. *How happy are we when a friend shows up unexpectedly at church?*

_____

_____

_____

_____

_____

_____

This man and his wife make us feel so welcomed. Though everyone in a church can greet visitors, some people have a real gift for hospitality. *How can we best do our part to embrace people at church?*

_____

_____

_____

_____

_____

_____

We learn that this is "Faith Promise Sunday," so they won't have a sermon. The lack of a lecture overjoys me. *Do we feel we need to hear a message for church to take place?*

_____

_____

_____

_____

_____

_____

Instead of a message, they explain the six ministries they support. Then members from the missions committee pray for these organizations and people. When they announce the pledge total, the congregation celebrates. *How does our church celebrate missions?*

_____

_____

_____

_____

_____

Hearing about the work of God's people to share his love fed my soul. I'm encouraged by a church that treats missions seriously and not as a minor add-on to a normally cash-strapped budget. *Do we make missions a priority?*

CHURCH #64: IS BIGGER ALWAYS BETTER?

This nontypical, nondenominational church enjoys a good amount of positive local buzz. Today is Mother's Day. I'm apprehensive because visiting a church on a holiday never provides a typical experience.

Two young women at the entrance to the parking lot smile and wave as we pull in. What a nice greeting. *What can we do at our church to help make a great first impression on others as they arrive?*

_____

_____

_____

_____

_____

Inside the facility I spot a lady wearing a T-shirt that suggests she's a greeter. Her broad smile beckons me. I ask for directions, and she's most helpful. *When people look at us, do we appear approachable or repelling?*

_____

_____

_____

_____

_____

With in-the-round seating, the worship team faces each other to get cues from their leader. Those closest have their backs to us. Though disconcerting, it's less like a performance and more worshipful. *How can we remember church isn't a concert?*

_____

_____

_____

_____

_____

_____

Today's also Ascension Sunday. With the focus on mothers, singing about Jesus's resurrection is the closest we'll get to acknowledging his ascension. *What does Jesus's return to heaven mean? How can we better celebrate his ascension?*

_____

_____

_____

_____

_____

_____

They conduct several baby dedications, striking a nice balance between the ceremony and celebrating the child, without dragging it into a too-long ritual. *While parents take the lead in raising their kids, how can we better support their efforts?*

_____

_____

_____

_____

_____

_____

The minister wraps up with an altar call of sorts, but he drones on, and I soon tune him out. *How can we keep our worship fresh and avoid the rut of repetition in our church services?*

_____

_____

_____

_____

_____

_____

A big church, they offer excellent teaching and music, with many programs and service opportunities, but they struggle providing community and connection. I leave spiritually full and emotionally hungry. *How can we help people leave church spiritually and emotionally filled?*

_____

_____

_____

_____

_____

_____

CHURCH #65: SHORT OF MEETING EXPECTATIONS

I met one of this church's staff at a speaker's conference. As we talked about the church's belief in the present-day power of the Holy Spirit, that same Holy Spirit nudged me to visit. At last we will.

Inside is a bustle of activity, which beckons us to the right, yet I spot a quiet, darkened sanctuary to my left. A woman glides up to direct us. *How observant are we to people needing assistance?*

_____

_____

_____

_____

_____

_____

It's time for the service to begin, but my friend from the speaker's conference dismisses my concern. "We don't start on time here." She smiles and gestures to the throng still behind us. *Is our church's starting time fact or fiction?*

_____

_____

_____

_____

_____

_____

Every song is new to me, and I struggle to mouth the words. The Bible says, "Sing a new song," not the ones we know and like. *What is our attitude toward singing new songs? What about our favorites?*

_____

_____

_____

_____

_____

_____

As we sing, one woman dances worshipfully off to the right, several more wave flags, and a few raise their hands as they sing. *How open are we to give God our physical worship?*

_____

_____

_____

_____

_____

_____

The minister talks about living expectantly. Imagine waking up each morning and asking God, "Daddy, what are we going to do today?" What a grand way to live life. *How can we live with this kind of expectation?*

_____

_____

_____

_____

_____

_____

After the closing song, prayer teams form up front. Gentle music produces a safe and holy place. Some people go forward for prayer. *What can we do to provide a safe prayer time that people will accept?*

_____

_____

_____

_____

_____

This church does many things right, but I expected more Holy Spirit presence. This is my fault for making false assumptions. *How should we respond when we don't get what we expect or assume?*

CHURCH #66, PART 1: GIFTS OF THE SPIRIT

Valued friends invite us to visit their church, which "operates in the gifts of the Spirit." My background is not charismatic, but I relish the opportunity to experience Holy Spirit power and bask in God's presence.

Many churches talk about the Holy Spirit, but their services leave little room for him to act. They keep him at a safe distance. *What role does the Holy Spirit play in our church services? In our daily lives?*

_____
_____
_____
_____
_____
_____

I'm hungry for God, thirsty for more. I can't wait for Sunday, counting down the days. Sadly, this attitude of church anticipation is mostly missing from my recent reality. *How much do we anticipate worshiping God? What needs to change?*

_____
_____
_____
_____
_____

Their website mentions the baptism of the Holy Spirit, speaking in tongues, the gifts of the Spirit, and supernatural manifestations. I'm terrified and excited. I expect God will stretch me. *How willing are we to let God work in us?*

_____

_____

_____

_____

_____

I still struggle visiting churches. Apprehension over the unknown roils in my gut. A dozen worries assault my mind. I suspect others also arrive at church filled with apprehension. *How can we help anxious people feel at ease?*

_____

_____

_____

_____

_____

Many raise their arms in praise, others sway gently with the melody, one respectfully dances her worship, and some wave worship flags. *How open are we to worship God through movement? Are we willing to be uncomfortable when others praise him?*

_____

_____

_____

_____

_____

_____

After about twenty minutes of singing, I think we're still on the first song. The endless iterations weary Candy, whereas I grow bored. *Does our worship of God push people away or draw us closer?*

_____

_____

_____

_____

_____

_____

With their minister gone, their service wasn't typical. I saw little evidence of the Holy Spirit. I'm disappointed. My experience didn't match what their website proclaims. *Do our church services align with what our marketing promises?*

_____

_____

_____

_____

_____

_____

_____

CHURCH #66, PART 2: A NORMAL SERVICE

Several months later we have a chance for a return visit to this same church. The opportunity to experience a normal service with their regular pastor should provide the chance to experience what we missed the first time.

The church moved since our first visit. An exterior sign guides us to the entrance, but that's it. We walk down a long corridor and eventually find an open door. *How easy is it for people to find us?*

_____

_____

_____

_____

_____

_____

We sing four songs, filling most of an hour. I try to worship God, but we don't connect. I should have prayed with greater intention for this service. *Who's to blame when we can't connect with God?*

_____

_____

_____

_____

_____

_____

As we sing, several people ease toward the pastor and surround him. They place their hands on him. Their lips move in quiet prayer. *Do we pray for our ministers before the service, during the service, or not at all?*

_____

_____

_____

_____

The pastor begins with prophecies and prayers for healing as the Holy Spirit directs him. *Do we let God's Spirit guide us to prophesy and pray for supernatural healing? If not, is he not speaking or are we not listening?*

_____

_____

_____

_____

The pastor says to not preach against other religions, but to preach Jesus. Too many people fail to follow his advice, suggesting why so many view Christians negatively. *Do we rant about what we're against or celebrate what we're for?*

_____

_____

_____

_____

_____

_____

When the minister shares a verse, I never see him glance at his notes. The text and reference gush forth as regular speech. *Do we know Scripture well enough to quote and cite it as normal dialogue?*

_____

_____

_____

_____

_____

_____

The Holy Spirit powerfully directed our time together through both the teaching pastor and the worship leader. I've seen few church services this Spirit-led. *Does the Holy Spirit direct what we do when we gather with other believers?*

CHURCH #67: SATELLITE CHURCH

We're off to visit another church, this time with family, the first visit for everyone. When they opened two years ago, they conducted a smart direct-mail campaign to the community. They're a portable church that meets at a nearby middle school.

The church is three-quarters of a mile away. We could walk but talk ourselves out of it. *Are we willing to attend a church near our home? Are we willing to walk there?*

___

___

___

___

___

___

___

They are a satellite location of an established church. Each site has a teaching pastor and worship team, with centralized governance and financial control. *How willing are we to try new ways to reach more people for Jesus?*

___

___

___

___

___

___

___

As we move inside the facility, two men interrupt their conversation to welcome us. *Are we willing to stop talking with people we know to meet those we don't?*

_____

_____

_____

_____

_____

_____

People chat with friends before the service begins. Soft music plays in the background. The atmosphere strikes a pleasing balance between sitting in stoic silence and an overwhelming rush of activity. *How can we best prepare to worship God?*

_____

_____

_____

_____

_____

_____

As we wait for the service, the interlude is pleasant. Though worshipful, the subdued ambience of the indirect lighting makes it hard to read the literature they gave us. *How can we best set the right mood for worship?*

_____

_____

_____

_____

_____

_____

The space fills. All age groups show up, but the demographics skew younger, with many families present. *What does the makeup of our church say about us? What does it foreshadow about our church's future?*

_____

_____

_____

_____

_____

_____

We learn about Breaking Bread, where three individuals or families meet three times in three months around a shared meal. This helps people get to know others and form connections. *What can we do to better connect with others?*

_____

_____

_____

_____

_____

During the message, I jot down a soundbite: "Know your community." This makes sense. If we're going to reach our neighbors, we must understand them. *How can we better know the people in our community?*

_____

_____

_____

_____

_____

The pastor provides a three-step process to engage people: 1) talk to them, 2) ask them a question, 3) invite them to do something (a meal, outing, or service opportunity). *What can we do to engage people?*

___

___

___

___

___

___

The service ends, and two things happen. Most people pick up their chair, collapse it, and stow it on a nearby rack. Others come up to talk. *What happens at our church when the service ends?*

___

___

___

___

___

___

I long to go to church in my community and attend with my neighbors, instead of driving several minutes to church in someone else's neighborhood and worshiping with other commuters. *How important is making spiritual connections where we live?*

_____

_____

_____

_____

_____

_____

_____

CHURCH #68: URBAN ON A MISSION

The website of this urban church says they're a multi-racial, multi-socio-economic relational community, where the homeless worship and support one another. I anticipate meeting people of other races and expect a service relevant to its inner-city neighborhood.

As we approach the building, others carry crockpots. Looks like a potluck. A shared meal is a powerful way to connect with others and build community. *What can we do to get to know others and create a sense of community?*

_____

_____

_____

_____

_____

_____

Two people welcome us before we enter the building and more greet us inside. They tell us two key pieces of information: the location of the sanctuary and directions to the restrooms. *What key information do visitors need to know?*

_____

_____

_____

_____

_____

_____

The crowd of white faces isn't the amalgamation of races promised. I don't spot anyone who looks homeless. Aside from location, it doesn't look like an urban church. *What can we do to make our churches more diverse and inclusive?*

_____

_____

_____

_____

_____

_____

As the minister concludes his message, he reminds us to pray for one person to lead to Jesus. *How can we do better at being expectant and ready to tell people about Jesus?*

_____

_____

_____

_____

_____

_____

In true potluck style, I take a bit of most everything. Good food, good fellowship, and good times. I like the way they do church. *What do we think church should be? What must we change to do church better?*

_____

_____

_____

_____

_____

_____

Throughout the day we suffer no awkward moments. These people welcome well. They're an engaging group, intentional about their faith and their life. *How can we live with greater kingdom intention?*

_____

_____

_____

_____

_____

I'm glad we stayed to eat with them and enjoy community instead of scooting out right away. *Do people at our church leave when the service concludes or tarry to talk and hang out?*

PART 2

OTHER CONSIDERATIONS

I have three more churches on my spreadsheet to visit. They've been languishing there for months. In addition, I have four more on my mental list. I consider adding them to my spreadsheet, but I never do.

We're doing a bad job at moving forward to visit these first three churches. I may be procrastinating. That means the next four will have to wait even longer. *How can we move from good intention to positive action?*

___

___

___

___

___

Visiting churches was my idea, not Candy's. She's been most supportive. I don't want to push past her willingness to cheerfully participate. *How can we make sure we don't wrongly impose our ideas or plans on others?*

___

___

___

___

___

I admit that I'm weary of visiting churches. I wonder if I should wrap up this undertaking. Therefore, I'll explore these next seven churches from afar. *How can we decide when to push forward on a project and when to conclude?*

_____

_____

_____

_____

_____

_____

_____

CHURCH #69: SUFFERING FROM A BAD RAP

On my list of seven churches is a church from a small conservative denomination. I've never met anyone who currently goes to one of this denomination's churches, but I have met people who *used* to go there.

These people left this church bruised and bloodied, rejected by those they used to worship with. Their church pushed them out over issues I consider trivial. *How can we disagree with people without causing them pain?*

_____

_____

_____

_____

_____

Every church has detractors. As frail humans, with a sinful nature, this will occur. But to meet only people this denomination hurt is troublesome. *How can we make sure we don't harm our church's reputation or the name of Jesus?*

_____

_____

_____

_____

_____

I want to visit and learn more. But I already know too much and couldn't go with an open mind. I must adjust my perspective. *When we have a bad attitude, do we seek God's help to correct it?*

_____

_____

_____

_____

_____

_____

CHURCH #70: UNPLANNED AND SPONTANEOUS

I once stumbled upon a group of Young Quakers online. Their faith, passion for community, and desire to make a difference in their world drew me in. I was intrigued and curious, but they had no gathering close by.

Casting a wider net for Quakers in general, I found a meeting nearby. They get together the first, third, and fifth Sundays of each month. *How open are we to not go to church every week?*

_____

_____

_____

_____

_____

_____

Another interesting difference is they have no minister. With no clergy to lead them, everyone can participate in an egalitarian manner. *How well would we function in a leaderless faith community as true equals?*

_____

_____

_____

_____

_____

_____

According to their website, their meetings are unplanned and spontaneous. I suspect they spend a lot of time listening to the Holy Spirit, reacting as appropriate. *How open are we to listen to the Holy Spirit?*

CHURCH #71: A MESSIANIC JEWISH CONGREGATION

Before *52 Churches*, we visited a Messianic Jewish church: Jews who believe in Jesus as their Jewish savior, mixing Hebrew tradition with Christian faith. Recalling our time with this first Messianic Jewish congregation, I add another one to my list.

Meeting Saturday evenings, the service at this first church involved time for worship and teaching. They concluded with a potluck, sharing food with a Jewish flair. *Besides a shared meal, how else can we foster spiritual community?*

_____

_____

_____

_____

_____

_____

With some parts of the service in Hebrew, worshiping God in another tongue brought a freshness to me. Their unfamiliar traditions strangely energized me. *How can we keep our relationship with God fresh and invigorating?*

_____

_____

_____

_____

_____

_____

Their worship space was in the basement of a Protestant church. This was ideal, since neither group used the facility at the same time. *In what creative ways can we find worship space for ourselves or provide it to others?*

_____

_____

_____

_____

_____

_____

_____

CHURCH #72: RESPECTED AND ESTEEMED

In addition to these three remaining churches on my spreadsheet is my mental list of four more. The first of these churches is the Salvation Army. Most people know the Salvation Army for their red donation kettles at Christmastime.

The Salvation Army addresses the needs of the homeless and provides disaster relief and humanitarian aid. They're also a church. Few people know this. *What would we think about being known as a service organization first and a church second?*

_____

_____

_____

_____

_____

_____

I think highly of the Salvation Army. I suspect most everyone does. Though I'm sure they aren't perfect, I've yet to hear anyone say a critical word. *What do people think about us? Our church? The Savior we represent?*

_____

_____

_____

_____

_____

The Salvation Army positively impacts their community and world. Helping one person at a time, they make a difference, serving as the hands and feet of Jesus. *How can we make our world better?*

CHURCH #73: A DEBATABLE DESTINATION

Next on my mental list of churches to visit sits a contentious consideration. It's Mormon, The Church of Jesus Christ of Latter-day Saints (LDS for short). I remain undecided if it's wise to visit or not.

I read that most Mormons consider themselves Christians, whereas most non-Mormon Christians don't. I suspect this conclusion, however, comes mostly from a lack of accurate information. *How can we form a nonjudgmental understanding about the faith journey of others?*

The Mormons Candy and I know exemplify Christian talk, behavior, and beliefs more so than a lot of other Christians we know. *Which do we esteem more, people who say they're Christian or those who act like it?*

Mormons hold to some beliefs that non-Mormons find strange. Yet, I suspect, the same holds true with every church. *How open are we to other spiritual practices? How sure are we of our own?*

_____

_____

_____

_____

_____

_____

_____

CHURCH #74: AN INTRIGUING MYSTERY

Another church is Anglican Catholic. They're also on my mental list of churches to visit. I know nothing about them or their faith practices. I expect their service to be much like Roman Catholic, but I'm not sure.

I'm curious and intrigued. I'm sure I can gather much to contemplate about our common faith and our varied worship practices. *What steps can we take to expand our understanding of worshiping God and embrace the faith journey of others?*

_____

_____

_____

_____

_____

_____

Unlike other streams of Christianity and other Protestant denominations, I've never met anyone who was Anglican Catholic—at least not that I'm aware of. *What do our friends know about our faith and which church we go to?*

_____

_____

_____

_____

_____

Lacking information about their practices, this church emerges for me with a mystical aura, but I doubt that's accurate. *What uninformed assumptions might we hold about others that we should seek to verify or correct?*

CHURCH #75: FATIGUE AND FEAR SET IN

Greek Orthodox sits fourth on my mental list of churches to visit. Like Anglican Catholic, I've never talked to anyone who was Greek Orthodox. Historically, I understand they split from the Roman Catholic Church about a thousand years ago.

What little I know about Greek Orthodox practices comes from what I've seen in movies and television. This is hardly an ideal source of information. *In what ways does the media incorrectly shape our views of spiritual practices we don't know?*

_____

_____

_____

_____

_____

_____

Inertia keeps me from visiting a nearby Greek Orthodox church. An element of fear over the unknown also conspires to keep me away. *How might inertia or fear hold us back from what God wants to teach us?*

_____

_____

_____

_____

_____

_____

A degree of church-visiting fatigue keeps me stagnant. Similar issues may keep others home on Sunday and thwart them from finding a faith community to plug into. *Are we part of a supportive faith community? If not, what should change?*

_____

_____

_____

_____

_____

_____

OUR HOME CHURCH

For *52 Churches*, we took a year off and visited a different Christian church every Sunday. Then we returned to our home church. For *More Than 52 Churches* we interspersed our visits with regular attendance at our home base.

Staying connected to our home church kept us anchored in spiritual community as we visited others. *What provides our spiritual anchor? If we don't have one, where can we look for it?*

_____

_____

_____

_____

_____

_____

Attending our home church required a fifteen-minute trip, driving past many other options that were more accessible and more inviting. *Why do we go to the church we do? Is it to meet our preferences or to advance God's kingdom?*

_____

_____

_____

_____

_____

_____

For years, I've longed to go to church in my community, worshiping and serving with my neighbors and family. *How important is it for us to worship in our community with our neighbors?*

_____

_____

_____

_____

_____

_____

After our first visit to Church #67, we returned the next week. We came back a third time, staying for their after-church meeting to learn more about their community. *How can we encourage first-time visitors to become regular attendees?*

_____

_____

_____

_____

_____

_____

Soon going to Church #67 turned into a habit. It was a good habit to form. *Not all habits are beneficial, so how can we discern the difference? Do we have a habit we should break?*

_____

_____

_____

_____

_____

_____

BONUS CONTENT: HOW TO BE AN ENGAGING CHURCH

The experiences I share in this book are *my* experiences. Others may have different observations. I'm an introvert, as is a slight majority of people. Even so, I doubt my reactions are unique to me or even to other introverts.

Whether introvert or extrovert, I've never talked with anyone who claimed they could visit a new church without some degree of anxiety. *How can the knowledge that visitors carry some unease better inform our interactions with them?*

_____

_____

_____

_____

_____

_____

_____

In visiting churches, I had a most supportive wife at my side. With her I stood much braver than I would have on my own. *Who can we invite to go with us on our spiritual journeys?*

_____

_____

_____

_____

_____

_____

_____

Visiting a church alone is even harder than going with a friend. It's easy to see why someone with even the best intentions of visiting will stay home. *Who can we invite to go to church with us?*

_____

_____

_____

_____

_____

_____

People hold to the Sunday schedule they know—whether staying home or attending church. Maintaining our norm is easier than trying something new. *What do we need to change in our Sunday routine?*

_____

_____

_____

_____

_____

_____

Churches that want to grow must do everything possible to make it less scary for a visitor to show up. Being welcoming is a start, but there's more. Churches must be likeable, even irresistible. *How can we become irresistible people?*

_____

_____

_____

_____

_____

_____

Tip 1: Make it Easy for Visitors

Most people today go online to find information about a church they're thinking of visiting. Therefore, having an attractive, up-to-date, and visitor-friendly website is essential. Don't make them search. They don't have much patience.

Some churches forego a website and try social media instead. But social media platforms can change their rules, restrict access, and even shut us down. *What impact would our church feel if we lost our social media presence?*

_____

_____

_____

_____

_____

_____

Our website must be attractive, be easy to navigate, and follow best practices. It needs a makeover every few years to not look dated. *What can we do to improve our church's website?*

_____

_____

_____

_____

_____

Make it easy for prospective visitors to contact our church with questions. This means listing a phone number and email address. Respond quickly to both. Most churches don't. *How can we help our church be more responsive to visitor questions?*

_____

_____

_____

_____

_____

_____

Tip 2: Create a Great Impression

When a visitor arrives at church, create a great first impression, building on their perception that began with our website. A website may encourage a person to visit a church, but it takes a personal connection to turn one-time visitors into returnees.

Some large churches have parking lot attendants to direct traffic and forward-thinking smaller churches have greeters in their parking lot to welcome visitors and answer questions. *What impression does our church make* before *people enter the building?*

_____

_____

_____

_____

_____

_____

Greet visitors at the building entrance with a smile, welcome them, and open the door. Greeters should focus on people they don't recognize. *Whether we're an official greeter or not, what can we do to better welcome visitors?*

_____

_____

_____

_____

_____

A positive welcome extends inside the building. Regardless of church size, seek ways to assist those who look confused. *What can we do to rescue a visitor who looks lonely or lost?*

_____

_____

_____

_____

_____

Tip 3: Greet Well

As mentioned in *52 Churches*, there are three opportunities to greet visitors: before the service, during the service, and after the service. Few churches do all three well and too many fail at each one.

Pre-service greetings can occur in the parking lot, at the front door, and inside the facility. In addition to official greeters, everyone should take part. *Regardless of how outgoing we are, what can we do to interact with visitors?*

_____

_____

_____

_____

_____

If there's a greeting during the service, we must be visitor-focused, not friend-focused. Make eye contact, smile, and offer a handshake. Share our name. Ask theirs. Now introduce them to someone else. *How can we better embrace visitors during the greeting time?*

_____

_____

_____

_____

_____

The final greeting occurs after the service. Before visitors scoot out, talk to them. Just be friendly. Seek a connection. Invite them to stay for any after-church activity. *How can we better connect with visitors after the service?*

_____

_____

_____

_____

_____

Engaging Church Summary

To grow, a church should engage with visitors. This starts with online information, helping them to decide to visit. It continues by making multiple good impressions when they arrive. It culminates with greeting them successfully before, during, and after the service.

Churches won't succeed in each area every time, but we should work to succeed in as many as possible, as often as possible. *What can we do to be more engaging as a church? As individuals?*

BONUS CONTENT: HOW TO GO TO CHURCH

For both visitors and regular attendees, three keys exist to having a successful, meaningful, and Spirit-filled church experience: attitude, prayer, and expectation. Following these steps can make most any church experience—despite its shortcomings—a positive one.

In going to church I've experienced both positive and negative outcomes, which often hinged on my attitude, prayer, and expectations—or the lack thereof. *Which of these three keys should we focus on to realize a more positive outcome at church?*

Tip 1: Attitude is Everything

If we approach church with a bad attitude, we shouldn't expect to enjoy our time there. It's foolish to assume a positive outcome if we hold a surly disposition.

When we approach church positively, our optimism will direct our attention to celebrate the noteworthy and give us the grace to overlook the not-so-great. *What can we do to go to church with an eager attitude? How can we encourage others to do the same?*

_____

_____

_____

_____

_____

_____

Tip 2: Prayer Is Essential

When Candy and I started visiting churches, we committed ourselves to a pre-church prayer each week. So significant were the benefits of these prayers that we continued the practice when we returned to our home church.

After several weeks, however, our pre-church prayer slipped into a rut, with us repeating the same tired phrases each time. *Are we willing to pray before church every Sunday? How can we avoid our prayers becoming routine?*

_____

_____

_____

_____

_____

_____

Tip 3: Expectations Form Experience

The foundation formed by prayer prepares us for the church service. It serves to shape expectations, which drives experience. Most of the time, positive expectations result in positive outcomes, while negative thinking produces negative experiences.

We say our pre-church prayer in faith, and we prove it from the activities that spring forth from our expectations. This is how we put faith into action. *If we don't like church, who's to blame: church, God, or us?*

_____

_____

_____

_____

_____

_____

Go to Church Summary

Whether visiting a new church or attending our home church, we should follow a wise strategy, remembering that attitude is everything, prayer is essential, and expectations form experience. Then we'll be ready to worship God and serve others.

When we go to church properly prepared, we can receive God's blessing and be a blessing to others. *What must we change to ensure we go to church with the right attitude, covered with prayer, and with godly expectations?*

_____

_____

_____

_____

_____

_____

THE NEXT STEPS

Another exploration of visiting churches has wrapped up, producing memories and insights. These can serve to move us forward in our spiritual journey, better prepared to worship God, serve others, and experience community.

Church means different things to different people, with our understanding of it evolving over time. The same applies to faith. Review your answers in this workbook. *How has your view of church grown? What changes should we make in how we put our faith into action?*

_____

_____

_____

_____

_____

_____

I hope the questions in this book have spurred a lot of great ideas. But without action, great ideas amount to nothing. *What are the top three things we want to start doing differently?*

_____

_____

_____

_____

_____

_____

When visiting churches, one person often made the difference between us feeling accepted and rejected. *In addition to changes we want to make in our own interactions with visitors, how can we encourage others to follow our example?*

_____

_____

_____

_____

_____

_____

_____

∽

If you liked *The More Than 52 Churches Workbook*, please leave a review online. Your review will help others discover this book and encourage them to read it too.

Thank you.

WHICH BOOK DO YOU WANT TO READ NEXT?

Other books in the Visiting Churches Series:

52 Churches

More Than 52 Churches

Visiting Online Church

Shopping for Church

The 52 Churches Workbook

For a list of all Peter's books, go to

PeterDeHaan.com/books.

ABOUT PETER DEHAAN

Peter DeHaan, PhD, wants to change the world one word at a time. His books and blog posts discuss God, the Bible, and church, geared toward spiritual seekers and church dropouts. Many people feel church has let them down, and Peter seeks to encourage them as they search for a place to belong.

But he's not afraid to ask tough questions or make religious people squirm. He's not trying to be provocative. Instead, he seeks truth, even if it makes people uncomfortable. Peter urges Christians to push past the status quo and reexamine how they practice their faith in every part of their lives.

Peter earned his doctorate, awarded with high distinction, from Trinity College of the Bible and Theological Seminary. He lives with his wife in beautiful Southwest Michigan and wrangles crossword puzzles in his spare time.

A lifelong student of Scripture, Peter wrote the 1,000-page website ABibleADay.com to encourage people to explore the Bible, the greatest book ever written. His popular blog, at PeterDeHaan.com, addresses biblical Christianity to build a faith that matters.

Read his blog, receive his newsletter, and learn more at PeterDeHaan.com.

BOOKS BY PETER DEHAAN

Visiting Churches Series

52 Churches

The 52 Churches Workbook

More Than 52 Churches

The More Than 52 Churches Workbook

Visiting Online Church

Shopping for Church

40-Day Bible Study Series

Dear Theophilus (the Gospel of Luke)

Acts Bible Study

Isaiah Bible Study

Minor Prophets Bible Study

Job Bible Study

Living Water (John)

Love Is Patient (1 and 2 Corinthians)

Revelation Bible Study

1, 2, & 3 John Bible Study

Hebrews Bible Study

James and Jude Bible Study

Matthew Bible Study

1 & 2 Peter Bible Study

Mark Bible Study

Holiday Celebration Devotional Series

The Advent of Jesus

The Passion of Jesus (Lent)

The Victory of Jesus (Easter)

The Ministry of Jesus

Thanksgiving with Jesus

New Year with Jesus

Bible Character Sketches Series

Women of the Bible

The Friends and Foes of Jesus

Old Testament Sinners and Saints

More Old Testament Sinners and Saints

Heroes and Heavies of the Apocrypha

200 Old Testament Sinners and Saints

Other Books

Elephant God

Jesus's Broken Church

Martin Luther's 95 Theses (formerly *95 Tweets*)

The Christian Church's LGBTQ Failure

Bridging the Sacred-Secular Divide (formerly *Woodpecker Wars*)

Beyond Psalm 150

How Big Is Your Tent?

For the latest list of all Peter's books, go to PeterDeHaan.com/books.

www.ingramcontent.com/pod-product-compliance
Lightning Source LLC
Chambersburg PA
CBHW072019110526
44592CB00012B/1368